ESSEX TYLER
Riding the Wave

photography Nigel Aird, Simon Cook, Steve Tanner

design Nick Harpley, satzooma

typeface Egyptienne F

Published by TG Publishing

www.essextyler.com

ISBN 978-1-5262-0063-1

楽

an unfinished quality,strength and vitality, with an essential spark of spontaneity

from *A Good Pot* by Christa Maria Herrmann

Of the four elements – water, fire, air and earth – water is the vital force in Essex Tyler's work. Not surprisingly, given that his identity as a surfer, sailor and fisherman bleeds in to his art.

As a painter, Essex brings together big liquid skies, the irascible Atlantic Ocean and the copper-stained cliffs of West Cornwall in landscapes that move one step beyond his contemporaries in capturing a quiet intensity, a kind of brooding – but a celebratory brooding.

Heron-blue skies weigh heavy on golden rocks that are bursting treasure chests – but this is not sweet earth. It spills out in rough coughs against the incessant forced medicine of the Atlantic Ocean. Sometimes the bronze of fiery earth leaks into the sky and stains it. Essex first established himself as a potter, so he knows the clays and metals that stain his paintings intimately. It is this translation of the physicality of clay forms and their firing into painting that makes his canvases so unique and powerful.

Raku pots, veined with cobalt, want to burst open like ripe fruit. The textures are smooth and burnished, with intricate cracks appearing by chance, a metaphor for life.

I have been a successful professional surfer, reared from an early age on the shape-shifting swells at Gwenver beach near Land's End. When I was a kid growing up in Cornwall, Essex was my surfing hero.

Gwenver was his local beach and he was in the elite class. He rode waves with Zen-like precision, the master of style, unshowy and graceful, with flashes of brilliance punctuated by perfectly timed maneouvres; elegant, sweeping turns on heaving stacks of water.

What separated Essex from the local standouts was his ability to tube ride on big, offshore days, taking off deep as a massively thick square lip tapped him on the shoulder out of curiosity but did not break on his back because he had slipped ahead of the game, his positioning and timing perfect. We younger surfers sat in the channel, watched and learned. The tube ride is the ultimate destination for every surfer, a place where time seems to stand still, a sensation not far removed from the meditative state sought by Asian philosophies that is also the psychological cauldron that fires excellent Raku pottery – the cauldron of imagination twinned with a cool detachment.

There is yin and yang to Essex's surfing: he can ride both short and long boards with ease, translating the power and torque of a six feet long slither of foam and fibreglass to the grace and glide of nine feet of board slotting straight into the historical tradition of longboarding. Within this tradition, following the Zen masters such as Dewey Weber and David Nuuiwha, Essex quickly mastered the noseride, where the rider has to link visualization and body movement to read the wave ahead of time, then apply weight, yet remain weightless, as all five toes – and ten if you can – are wrapped around the very tip of the board in a moment of pure balance.

This is not a flourish or a decoration, but a point in which one stands in a processional line, starting with the ancient Hawaiian tradition, reaching through post-war Southern California and spreading to all longboard stylists, all the way to Cornwall, the California of the UK.

It takes both grit and skill to rewrite the historical dance moves of the heyday of Californian longboard surfing and bring them into the pressure-cooker of the present without looking awkward. Especially as those darned Californians learned in warm water under sultry skies with perfectly peeling pointbreak waves in what they call a 'climate', where Essex honed his moves in often freezing cold, windblown, choppy conditions wrapped head to toe in neoprene and in the cold mist of West Cornish 'weather'.

I've watched Essex surfing on big greasy green waves all around the south coast of Cornwall, just under the big toe of the foot of county dipped in the Atlantic turbine, setting up a crisp bottom turn, adopting great posture, flexing low into outlandish re-entries, followed by rifling moves all the way to the shoreline, everything linked and coordinated. And now, this same string of events passes from head and heart to brush and canvas, with paint as the medium rather than the green Atlantic Ocean. In each arena liquidity is key – flow, movement, acceleration and pause, timing and placement.

The techniques of Raku pottery are not dissimilar to those of Zen Buddhism – intense heat firing and then cooling outside the kiln. Zen takes you straight to the red-hot heart of an object or a perception, an idea or a feeling, and then reduces it through a swift switch to intense contemplation.

This is caught in Zen koans – parables that burn with penetrating description and finish on a cool note of contemplation. Soyen Shaku, the Zen teacher who first brought Zen Buddhism to America, where Beat poets such as Allen Ginsberg and Gary Snyder eagerly adopted the teachings and practices, said *My heart burns like fire but my eyes are as cold as dead ashes.* In other words, an experience ignites but a subsequent contemplation creates reflective distance.

Essex knows this intuitively from Raku techniques but has successfully translated this across to his paintings. It is as if he has caught the world on fire with its toes dipped into a cold sea producing instant contemplation, so that impulse and reflection are caught at one and the same moment on the canvas.

Zen Buddhism prides itself on such a concentrated collision of body and mind, or instinct and reflection. Living in the present in a sense eradicates time, for there is no mindless wandering to recollection, and no fruitless future guesswork. "This state of mind is when you make your best art," admits Essex, "mindful, not mindless." This is when that current runs through you, the spirit bursts into flame, and you are fully absorbed, a state that translates in equal measure to Essex's pottery and painting, his fishing and sailing.

As a sailor, Essex (who owns a 1910 Salcombe Pilot Cutter) knows what it is like to sit on the skin of the ocean still as a bird while all around seems to boil. As a deep sea fisherman he recalls the grind of gruelling days and nights out in the Bay of Biscay, working a shoal – but also the pride of bringing in a fresh catch of tuna, returning to safe harbour in Newlyn on adrenalin overdrive, only to head for a grinding head-high surf before the pale body of exhaustion set in and the red body had to recuperate.

There's a wild freedom to Essex's work that mirrors a love and knowledge of the sea. A sea stirred overnight from glassy calm into a white-tipped frenzy is caught at its peak, the weather rushing in like a big tide, to dip and kiss the bronzed earthly world with its blessings and curses, and move off hurriedly: now wild, now eerily calm.

Essex also captures the calm geometry at the centre of these elaborate weather changes in his pots, celebrating more than a sense of place, to mirror a sense of movement around place. The pot is the *omphalos* – the still centre of the turning world, a piece of earth shaped, fired and glazed into culture with a mystery at its centre – an empty space to be left empty.

Pots may have been made originally for practical purposes, but when they become objects of beauty their aesthetic was partly due to the fact that they sit guarding an empty space.

There are tidal layers, repeated on canvas and clay, like the surfer's paddling motion, moving one presence smoothly over another. There are abstract boats sitting on the seaskin, ready to be tipped over, then there is the safety of harbour, temporarily tethered to feed the domestic imagination, where *terroir* – the very smell and taste of the place – replaces terror.

Essex's work appears effortless, but of course there is serious labour involved. He also has an acute eye to market other artists, a strong business head. From Essex's home in Mousehole, where he lives with his gorgeous wife Clare and two outgoing boys, Oscar and Charlie, you can overlook the old cobbled harbour – and across Mounts Bay, surf sometimes cleanly refracting around the south coast with feathering sea spray from a stiff northerly wind. The Tyler Gallery is just below the garden, buzzing with contemporary works of painting, pottery, sculpture and jewellery.

Squeezed between a maze of tiny streets, there is something indefinable, even magical, about Mousehole. Set at the edge of the rugged landscape of wild moorland, prehistoric remains and haunting ruins of the once-great tin and copper mining industries, Mousehole has a distinctive Mediterranean feel and cultural sophistication that sets it apart from its surroundings.

Many of the shops, galleries and restaurants capture this paradoxical down-home or earthy sophistication – the sort that attracts tourists who do not want the tawdry display of Newquay or even St Ives.

Mousehole is also a gateway to a host of surf breaks. From Gwenver through Sennen Cove to Porthcurno, quartz sands and granite cliffs skirt the sea, and you'll find some of the finest beaches and most dramatic coastline in Britain. Sitting outside the breaking surf out to sea and looking back at the vaulting rocks, surfers can take in dramatic landscapes equal to any in the world at the same time as experiencing the unique secret of the 'rainbow rinse' – on a windy, offshore day with a good swell, the water blows back off the wave and you sit there as the rainbow arcs over you in a private, psychedelic cave. The moment is deeply enhanced as a cormorant pops up, a seal looks you straight in the eye, or a dolphin suddenly appears and breaches. You pop your head underwater and you can hear the clicks of the pod communicating, probably discussing the state of the currents or how ungainly these humans look when they surf!

West Cornwall, or strictly Penwith, is the end of the line, where the train stops and the crowds thin. It rarely gets overwhelmed by the weight of summer tourist traffic and preserves an unpretentious, rugged feel.

Isolation generates a strong community spirit, but it can sometimes feel intimidating, dwarfed by Stone, Bronze and Iron Age antiquity and post-industrial mining ruins. Everywhere the once-molten grey bedrock breaks through the surface of the land frustrating attempts at cultivation. Then the spring rises, days lengthen, the gorse flickers and flowers, the heather and foxgloves blossom and the surf warms up. The pina colada – pineapple and coconut – smell of the gorse pervades the air.

The swallows have arrived and are dipping at speed, catching insects on the fly, there is a distant cuckoo and an adder slithers out right at your feet. The primrose clumps have thickened and beam out from the springy grass. Red kites hover, returning from the edge of extinction.

But Essex's love of this familiar terrain is increased through travel with surfboard and sail. He knows that the world is still brimming with empty surf spots, waiting to be ridden.

I've been lucky enough to travel with Essex. We surfed together in the Canary Islands, sailing on the Norwegian Blue, a friends' 42 feet yacht, hand-built with a five inch steel hull as icebreaker, designed ultimately to go north towards the Arctic Circle.

The Canaries was a great place for skipper Woody and surf guide Janus Howard to test the waters. Essex and I were eager to sample Los Lobos, a thrilling volcanic bottom pointbreak, punching down a sharp island reef for 300 metres, just outside Corralejo, Fuerteventura. This is the 'Hawaii of the Atlantic'.

On a brisk east wind the wave faces at Los Lobos heap up, grinding through the tides. The waves were breaking close to shore with tight, claustrophobic, long, clawing rides. The water was a rich Prussian blue, with a range of purples surfacing outback, and dark greens over the urchins inside. I can picture Essex one-hand-clapping lips in Zen style, and disappearing in and out of tubes. There were tight kick-outs as the shallow reef formed polka dots along the inside. In hollow pockets Essex sat low and deep, coolly caverned, before turning the whole board into a light, flexible and responsive dolphin-like animal, cracking out tail turns.

At dusk, the water turned plum coloured and each wave's own routine stood proud in our minds. Back on the yacht we celebrated the best surf of the trip and traded jokes about wipeouts. Unlike the meditative state of riding a wave, where the mind is cleared, the wipeout is a double-edged sword, the sharp reef ready to lacerate your skin, the mind trying to will away the inevitable. But when survived, they provide therapy through laughter – the kind of belly laughter that doubles you over so that you cannot catch your breath.

Essex loaned me Ernest Hemingway's *The Old Man and the Sea* on that trip. All ocean lovers can relate to the old fisherman who always thought of the sea as *la mar* which is what people call her in Spanish when they love her… as feminine and as something that gave or withheld great favours, and if she did wild or wicked things it was because she could not help them. Here I learned not only that Essex was a man of the sea, a reader, a great cook,but also modest, honest and easily able to share wisdom that I absorbed wholeheartedly.

ESSEX
SX

"When a set of waves comes through, you have to make a choice about which one to catch. When you get the wave it has peaks and it has troughs. It's a metaphor for life: there are peaks and troughs, high and lows. It's just a case of riding it through to the end. The secret is to hang in there."

Essex knows about the grind of the hard times, days at sea in a cauldron of storms in the Irish Sea, the creeping exhaustion of wicked winters in Cornwall. But he also knows about the healing power of water, best captured when having a relaxing barbeque at the beach with his family watching his boys standing proud and learning to surf. The same place planted the seed in Essex when he first trimmed a green face at Sennen aged six, coincidently the time he started to make pots, an immediate flowering of surfing as art.

Essex's dad, Chris Tyler, was a first generation Sennen surfer in the 1960s, when Britain's most southwesterly beach, two miles from Lands End, was merely a tight-knit fishing village with no car park. These surfers injected a new lifestyle to West Cornwall, amidst a social revolution where a freethinking generation flowered into vibrant alternative scenes.

A Mousehole trawlerman and great surfer, Chris Tyler had been making exploratory trips to Morocco and had a shot in *Surfer* magazine riding North Africa's magical waves. Chris was a pioneer at the deepwater breaks around Taghazoute, where speedy 200 metre-long rides are common. Locally, Chris was immersed in the growing surfing contest circuit and had a vision to open a surfing village to give people a little piece of the beauty of Cornwall. In 1974, he bought the land at an old RAF camp-come-holiday-centre near Land's End with a business partner. Complete with chalets, apartments, caravans, a pool, restaurant, bar and discotheque, Chris created *Skewjack Surf Village*.

Skewjack enticed a few national newspapers to send journalists to pen articles, and featured on the *BBC Holiday Show* in 1976. Chris had created a beating heart for both locals and holidaymakers and employed local surfers as lifeguards and instructors. This coincided with Penwith District Council forming a lifeguard service at the main Penwith beaches, and making a concerted effort to give the head jobs to locals. So began a history of beach employees who cared tirelessly for their office because it was home and they were driven to safeguard the surrounding beauty.

Steve Jamieson, the longtime head lifeguard at Sennen and Gwenver (starting in 1976) explains, "I love the variety here. Over the years we've seen so much, from adders, vultures, minks, pelicans, sharks, whales and dolphins, and to have been part of that is so fulfilling. Nothing can match living here. And what has been so rewarding has been educating the youngsters about the place and seeing them growing up into good all-round watermen and women."

Growing up at Skewjack, Essex (who was born in 1973) and his brother Cassius started surfing at such a young age that they quickly became two of the best junior surfers in Britain, known for their 'cool California' blonde hair and free flowing, radical styles. I got a lot of inspiration from watching them. Essex is only five years older than me, but this is a big gap when you are younger and for me his surfing always bought the mustard to the table.

"The whole Skewjack thing was great because we would have custom car shows, contests, live music and video nights. After a big breakfast we would head off down to Sennen in the *VW* camper van with all the people that had come down to stay and learn to surf. Lots of them fell for the place and ended up moving down to the area and still live here today." West Penwith was a magnet for a certain type of outgoing breed, inspired by the clean air and stark scenery.

"I remember an amazing summer of surf in 1981 when I had a 4′ 11″ *Ocean Magic* twin-fin swallow tail. It absolutely flew. It was totally different to what everyone else was riding at the time. I could rip it up on that board. It was probably the smallest surfboard in the country back then. People were starting to ride quite radical boards, but this was really ahead of the game. Gwenver back then was so quiet. It could be empty even on the best summer days. Right up until the late 1980s you could camp for 50 pence a night at the top of the hill."

Essex's surfing hero in the 1980s was Newlyn-raised Harvey Hoare, who used to take Essex and Cassius to surf competitions. Harvey was an explosive and lanky twin-fin expert with a flair for tube riding at the hallowed reef break at Porthleven on the south coast. His style was based loosely on that of the Australian four-times World Champion Mark Richards.

Speed and flow were punctuated by long swooping bottom turns and tight radical top turns. Throughout all the critical manoeuvering arms were splayed out pelican-like. Harvey was the epitome of the region's underground feel. In fact, a defining feature of Penwith is that very few of the more talented surfers have been interested in following the path of professional surfing. Introspection replaces competition.

The ideology of fashion and show is replaced by a search for the eternal return: a desire to enjoy the essence of life immersed in nature. Gwenver has always had this 'back to roots' culture and feel. My dad, Alan 'Fuz' Bleakley, who first surfed in 1965 and grew up in the Newquay scene, remembers surfaris to Nanjizal, Porthcurno, Sennen and Gwenver as like trips to the Wild West, where a frontier spirit could be felt.

"Harvey had loads of style," says Essex. Style matters for Essex. He oozes style, in his personality, the way he surfs and the way he throws pots and paints. It was no surprise that Essex was asked to feature as a 'local surf hero' in Carl Prechezer's film *Blue Juice* in 1995, showcasing Welsh sensation Catherine Zeta Jones. Former British Junior Champion Jamie Owen did the surfing sequences, doubling as lead character JC, in the Canary Islands. But most of the film was shot in Mousehole, Newlyn, Gwithian and St Ives.

Essex sports a wry smile when telling these stories, but his feet are firmly planted in the present. No nostalgia here. What I really admire about Essex is his acceptance and celebration that surfing, tourism and art are all part of the business of Cornwall. Every single piece of his artwork is brimming with a life lived in the moment.

“A blank canvas is like an empty wave,” he says, “ready to be surfed.” Essex paints like he surfs: graceful, long and natural arcs and lines, layer upon layer. Above all, he is a man of expressive colour that traps light. His surfing folded manouevre after manouevre into the folding wave, like trying to pack a box with water that keeps on collapsing around you. This results in the surfer bringing air into the ride that is in turn packed in to the folding wave. The appearance is one of effortless mastery.

So with Essex's art – he folds light and air into the clay and paint as he builds a body of work. And this light shines forth as the genie of the work, trapped until the lamp is caressed (cared for) and then revealed in appreciation.

"Painting is like surfing. You do not get anywhere before you have mastered the basics – spot the best waves, paddle out using the rip currents, take off at the point of maximum energy, bottom turn, tube ride, exit with style." But, of course, after that, spontaneous and sometimes unintentional movements can produce poetry on the waveface.

Essex uses oils, acrylics, beeswax and marble dust. Colours, tones and textures are repeated over and over to work as building blocks, so that improvisation becomes possible. Paint is pushed and pulled around the canvas, leaving traces that are tethers, tracks for the eye to follow upward, across, to rest finally on a deceptively still object, a symbol of shelter not just at the heart of the storm but also at the heart of the calm. For one of painting's key purposes is to provide shelter from the anaesthetising calm that is the pervasive blandness produced by a mundane culture.

A current new work brilliantly captures the glare of the low sun over red ground, escarpments that curve like boat hulls moving overland to Iron Age villages. It's as if there is a muttering from old Cornish mining merchants as they trade for Saharan gold and Egyptian riches with Berbers and Phoenicians. The very tip of West Cornwall must have seemed like the world's end to the ancients as the sun died and went to its overnight grave.

Essex brings beauty into everything he does. It was no surprise he was attracted to a Japanese artform, Raku pottery. There is a tradition of bringing beauty into everything in Japan, from building to making tea to social manners. Raku was the chosen pottery for the tea ceremony. Past and present blend seamlessly, so that even the Japanese factory workers making televisions talk of the spirits in the tube. Following a Shinto philosophy, whole temple complexes are completely rebuilt every 20 years in accordance with principles of purity and renewal. Many traditional habits pervade everyday Japanese life, from an emphasis on purification to an obsession with austere aesthetics and the celebration of the cherry blossom.

Raku Pottery (楽焼き Raku-Yaki) was developed in the early 1500s. Raku (楽) literally means 'felicity', signifying enjoyment of freedom. It was the favoured ceremonial teaware of the Zen Buddhist masters because of its undecorated humility. Ironically, Raku is hardly watertight, only holding liquid for a short period. It is pottery without utility or function, fired with lead-based glazes, producing unpredictable works of wonder. It is thrown with a wheel, which gives it a slightly uneven shape and style. The firing process is daring, a dramatic trial by fire.

A once-fired (bisque), unglazed pot is first coated with glaze and placed into the kiln, then heated at a fast rate. This often causes the pot to explode. If the pot survives this shock, it is blessed, glowing like a hot coal in a rainstorm, the glaze melting into a sheet of liquid glass.

The potter uses tongs to remove the glowing pot, the severe temperature change causing cracks in the glaze. These cracks are highly prized characteristics. The pot is placed directly into an airtight container filled with the artist's secret recipe, which turns the naked clay foot black and highlights the cracks in the glaze.

Sometimes the pot is plunged into cold water for greater effect. Imagine a flaming dawn burning your eyes, then jumping into an ice-cold sea with a new swell with an offshore wind fanning the flames.

Importantly it is believed that the spirit of the maker is embodied in the form and revealed at the foot, which is traditionally left naked (unglazed). It is believed that if we are alert to ourselves, in contemplating the Raku form we will recognize in it our own spirit and meaning. While the glazes in Raku are typically lapis, aqua and amethyst, Essex's pots seem glazed in reflected light from the ocean: seagrey, seablue and seagreen, contrasting with an earthy graphite. It's as if they hold cold currents and tidal layers. Others show a fiery sun and an icy moon, or a thicket of sea mist swallowing a cobalt blue sky. I have one in my kitchen that I once traded for a surfboard. It's like an atomic sky reflecting the colour explosion of the sea below.

Essex's experiences of surfing permanently feed the pots – peeling waves, translucent walls and transparent peaks close to hulking cliffs. He admits that the juxtapositions of blues are sea-like, making sense of surfing's marriage with art and the code that this unlocks:

"When I'm paddling out I like to spot the shapes and patterns of water moving," he says. "But when you make a pot, you never know how it will turn out. That's the beauty of Raku. That's the unpredictable spirit of it."